50 Restaurant Food Recipes for Home

By: Kelly Johnson

Table of Contents

- Classic Caesar Salad
- Beef Wellington
- Spaghetti Carbonara
- Chicken Alfredo
- Margherita Pizza
- Lobster Bisque
- Chicken Parmesan
- Shrimp Scampi
- Stuffed Bell Peppers
- Filet Mignon
- Eggplant Parmesan
- Thai Green Curry
- BBQ Ribs
- Beef Stroganoff
- Chicken Tikka Masala
- Clam Chowder
- Pad Thai
- Beef Tacos
- Mushroom Risotto
- Salmon Teriyaki
- Lasagna
- Chicken Marsala
- Greek Salad
- Peking Duck
- Shrimp and Grits
- Teriyaki Chicken
- Butternut Squash Soup
- Beef Bourguignon
- Chicken Enchiladas
- Vegetable Tempura
- Lobster Mac and Cheese
- Coq au Vin

- Pappardelle with Bolognese
- Moroccan Lamb Tagine
- Ratatouille
- Burrata with Tomatoes and Basil
- Prawn Curry
- French Onion Soup
- Baked Ziti
- Duck Confit
- Spicy Tuna Tartare
- Stuffed Mushrooms
- Chicken Cacciatore
- Creamy Tomato Basil Soup
- Grilled Octopus
- Enchiladas Verde
- Shrimp Fettuccine Alfredo
- Stuffed Acorn Squash
- Beef and Broccoli Stir-Fry
- Lobster Roll

Classic Caesar Salad

Ingredients:

- 1 large head of Romaine lettuce, chopped
- 1 cup Caesar dressing
- 1 cup croutons
- 1/2 cup freshly grated Parmesan cheese
- Optional: 1 cup grilled chicken or anchovies

Instructions:

1. In a large bowl, toss the chopped Romaine lettuce with Caesar dressing until evenly coated.
2. Add croutons and toss gently.
3. Sprinkle with grated Parmesan cheese.
4. Top with grilled chicken or anchovies if using.
5. Serve immediately.

Enjoy your salad!

Beef Wellington

Ingredients:

- 1.5 lbs beef tenderloin (center-cut)
- Salt and pepper, to taste
- 2 tbsp olive oil
- 8 oz mushrooms, finely chopped
- 2 tbsp unsalted butter
- 2 cloves garlic, minced
- 1/4 cup dry white wine
- 4 oz pâté (optional)
- 1 sheet puff pastry, thawed
- 1 egg, beaten

Instructions:

1. Preheat oven to 425°F (220°C).
2. Season beef with salt and pepper. Sear in olive oil over high heat until browned. Let cool.
3. Sauté mushrooms and garlic in butter until moisture evaporates. Add wine and cook until dry. Cool.
4. Spread pâté (if using) over beef. Top with mushroom mixture.
5. Wrap beef in puff pastry, sealing edges. Brush with beaten egg.
6. Bake for 25-30 minutes, or until pastry is golden and beef reaches desired doneness. Rest before slicing.

Spaghetti Carbonara

Ingredients:

- 12 oz (340 g) spaghetti
- 2 tbsp olive oil
- 4 oz (115 g) pancetta or guanciale, diced
- 3 large eggs
- 1 cup (100 g) freshly grated Parmesan cheese
- 2 cloves garlic, minced
- Salt and freshly ground black pepper, to taste
- Fresh parsley, chopped (optional, for garnish)

Instructions:

1. Cook spaghetti in a large pot of salted boiling water until al dente. Reserve 1 cup of pasta water, then drain the pasta.
2. In a large skillet, heat olive oil over medium heat. Add pancetta and cook until crispy. Remove from skillet and set aside.
3. In the same skillet, add garlic and sauté briefly until fragrant. Remove from heat.
4. In a bowl, whisk together eggs, Parmesan cheese, salt, and pepper.
5. Add the drained pasta to the skillet with garlic. Toss to coat in the residual oil.
6. Remove the skillet from heat and quickly toss in the egg mixture, adding a little reserved pasta water as needed to create a creamy sauce.
7. Stir in the cooked pancetta.
8. Serve immediately, garnished with fresh parsley if desired.

Enjoy your creamy Spaghetti Carbonara!

Chicken Alfredo

Ingredients:

- 12 oz (340 g) fettuccine
- 2 tbsp olive oil
- 2 chicken breasts, sliced
- Salt and pepper, to taste
- 3 cloves garlic, minced
- 1 cup heavy cream
- 1 cup (100 g) grated Parmesan cheese
- 2 tbsp unsalted butter
- Fresh parsley, chopped (optional, for garnish)

Instructions:

1. Cook fettuccine in salted boiling water until al dente. Drain and set aside.
2. Heat olive oil in a skillet over medium heat. Season chicken with salt and pepper, then cook until no longer pink. Remove and set aside.
3. In the same skillet, add garlic and sauté until fragrant.
4. Stir in heavy cream and butter, cooking until the sauce thickens slightly.
5. Remove from heat and mix in Parmesan cheese until smooth.
6. Add cooked fettuccine and chicken to the sauce, tossing to coat.
7. Garnish with fresh parsley if desired. Serve immediately.

Enjoy your creamy Chicken Alfredo!

Margherita Pizza

Ingredients:

For the Dough:

- 2 1/4 tsp (1 packet) active dry yeast
- 1 1/2 cups warm water (110°F/45°C)
- 4 cups all-purpose flour
- 2 tbsp olive oil
- 1 tsp sugar
- 1 tsp salt

For the Toppings:

- 1 cup tomato sauce (preferably San Marzano or Italian-style)
- 8 oz (225 g) fresh mozzarella cheese, sliced
- 1/2 cup grated Parmesan cheese
- Fresh basil leaves
- 2 tbsp olive oil
- Salt and freshly ground black pepper, to taste

Instructions:

1. **Prepare the Dough:**
    - In a small bowl, dissolve yeast and sugar in warm water. Let sit for about 5 minutes until foamy.
    - In a large bowl, mix flour and salt. Make a well in the center and pour in the yeast mixture and olive oil.
    - Mix until a dough forms, then knead on a floured surface for about 8-10 minutes, or until smooth and elastic.
    - Place the dough in a lightly oiled bowl, cover with a damp cloth, and let rise in a warm place for about 1-2 hours, or until doubled in size.
2. **Prepare the Pizza:**
    - Preheat your oven to 475°F (245°C). If using a pizza stone, preheat it in the oven.
    - Punch down the dough and divide it into 2 equal portions. Roll out each portion on a floured surface to your desired thickness.
    - Transfer the rolled-out dough to a pizza peel or baking sheet lined with parchment paper.
    - Spread a thin layer of tomato sauce over the dough, leaving a small border around the edges.
    - Arrange the fresh mozzarella slices evenly on top of the sauce.

- Sprinkle with grated Parmesan cheese and a drizzle of olive oil. Season with salt and pepper.
3. **Bake the Pizza:**
    - Bake in the preheated oven for 10-15 minutes, or until the crust is golden and the cheese is melted and bubbly.
    - Remove from the oven and immediately top with fresh basil leaves.
4. **Serve:**
    - Slice and serve the pizza hot.

Enjoy your homemade Margherita Pizza!

Lobster Bisque

Ingredients:

- 2 lobsters (1.5 lbs each), cooked and shelled (reserve shells)
- 2 tbsp butter
- 1 onion, chopped
- 2 cloves garlic, minced
- 1 carrot, chopped
- 1 celery stalk, chopped
- 1/4 cup tomato paste
- 1 cup white wine
- 4 cups seafood or chicken stock
- 1 cup heavy cream
- 1 tbsp flour (optional, for thickening)
- 2 tbsp brandy (optional)
- Salt and freshly ground black pepper, to taste
- Fresh parsley, chopped (for garnish)

Instructions:

1. **Prepare the Lobster:**
    - Remove meat from lobster shells and chop into bite-sized pieces. Set aside.
    - Crush the shells slightly and set aside.
2. **Make the Base:**
    - In a large pot, melt butter over medium heat. Add onion, garlic, carrot, and celery. Cook until softened.
    - Stir in tomato paste and cook for 2 minutes.
3. **Add Liquids and Shells:**
    - Add wine and scrape up any browned bits. Simmer for 2-3 minutes.
    - Add lobster shells and stock. Simmer for 20-30 minutes to infuse flavors.
4. **Blend and Strain:**
    - Remove shells and vegetables. Use an immersion blender to puree the soup, or carefully blend in batches.
    - Strain through a fine mesh sieve to remove any remaining solids.
5. **Finish the Bisque:**
    - Return soup to the pot. Stir in heavy cream and brandy (if using). Adjust thickness with flour if desired.
    - Season with salt and pepper. Simmer for 5-10 minutes, until heated through.
6. **Serve:**
    - Add lobster meat to the soup just before serving. Garnish with fresh parsley.

Enjoy your creamy Lobster Bisque!

Chicken Parmesan

Ingredients:

- 4 boneless, skinless chicken breasts
- Salt and pepper, to taste
- 1 cup all-purpose flour
- 2 large eggs, beaten
- 1 1/2 cups breadcrumbs
- 1 cup grated Parmesan cheese
- 1 cup marinara sauce
- 1 1/2 cups shredded mozzarella cheese
- 1/4 cup chopped fresh basil (optional)
- 1/4 cup olive oil

Instructions:

1. **Prepare the Chicken:**
   - Preheat oven to 375°F (190°C).
   - Season chicken breasts with salt and pepper. Dredge in flour, then dip in beaten eggs, and coat with breadcrumbs mixed with Parmesan cheese.
2. **Cook the Chicken:**
   - Heat olive oil in a large skillet over medium heat. Cook chicken until golden and crispy, about 4-5 minutes per side. Transfer to a paper-towel-lined plate.
3. **Assemble the Dish:**
   - Place chicken breasts in a baking dish. Spoon marinara sauce over each piece.
   - Sprinkle shredded mozzarella cheese on top.
4. **Bake:**
   - Bake in preheated oven for 20-25 minutes, or until cheese is melted and bubbly and chicken is cooked through.
5. **Garnish:**
   - Garnish with fresh basil if desired. Serve with pasta or a side salad.

Enjoy your Chicken Parmesan!

Shrimp Scampi

Ingredients:

- 1 lb (450 g) large shrimp, peeled and deveined
- 8 oz (225 g) linguine or spaghetti
- 4 tbsp unsalted butter
- 3 tbsp olive oil
- 4 cloves garlic, minced
- 1/4 cup dry white wine
- 1/4 cup freshly squeezed lemon juice (about 1 lemon)
- 1/4 cup chopped fresh parsley
- 1/4 tsp red pepper flakes (optional, for heat)
- Salt and freshly ground black pepper, to taste
- Lemon wedges (for serving)

Instructions:

1. **Cook the Pasta:**
   - Cook linguine or spaghetti according to package instructions until al dente. Reserve 1/2 cup of pasta water, then drain.
2. **Cook the Shrimp:**
   - While pasta is cooking, heat butter and olive oil in a large skillet over medium heat.
   - Add garlic and cook until fragrant, about 1 minute.
   - Add shrimp, red pepper flakes (if using), salt, and pepper. Cook until shrimp are pink and opaque, about 2-3 minutes per side. Remove shrimp from skillet and set aside.
3. **Make the Sauce:**
   - In the same skillet, pour in white wine and lemon juice. Scrape up any browned bits from the bottom of the pan. Simmer for 2-3 minutes until slightly reduced.
4. **Combine:**
   - Return shrimp to the skillet. Add cooked pasta and toss to combine, adding a bit of reserved pasta water if needed to loosen the sauce.
5. **Finish and Serve:**
   - Stir in chopped parsley and adjust seasoning with salt and pepper.
   - Serve immediately with lemon wedges on the side.

Enjoy your Shrimp Scampi!

Stuffed Bell Peppers

Ingredients:

- 4 large bell peppers (any color)
- 1 lb (450 g) ground beef or turkey
- 1 cup cooked rice (white or brown)
- 1 cup marinara sauce
- 1/2 cup onion, chopped
- 2 cloves garlic, minced
- 1 cup shredded cheese (cheddar or mozzarella)
- 1 tsp dried oregano
- 1/2 tsp dried basil
- Salt and pepper, to taste
- 2 tbsp olive oil

Instructions:

1. **Prepare the Peppers:**
   - Preheat oven to 375°F (190°C).
   - Cut the tops off the bell peppers and remove seeds and membranes. Lightly brush the outside of the peppers with olive oil.
2. **Cook the Filling:**
   - Heat olive oil in a skillet over medium heat. Sauté onion and garlic until soft.
   - Add ground beef or turkey, cooking until browned. Drain excess fat.
   - Stir in cooked rice, marinara sauce, oregano, basil, salt, and pepper. Cook for another 5 minutes.
3. **Stuff the Peppers:**
   - Fill each bell pepper with the meat mixture, pressing down gently to pack it in.
   - Place stuffed peppers upright in a baking dish.
4. **Bake:**
   - Bake in preheated oven for 25-30 minutes.
   - Remove from oven, sprinkle with shredded cheese, and return to bake for an additional 5 minutes, or until cheese is melted and bubbly.
5. **Serve:**
   - Let cool slightly before serving.

Enjoy your Stuffed Bell Peppers!

Filet Mignon

Ingredients:

- 2 filet mignon steaks (6-8 oz each)
- Salt and freshly ground black pepper, to taste
- 2 tbsp olive oil
- 2 cloves garlic, minced
- 2 tbsp unsalted butter
- Fresh rosemary or thyme (optional, for garnish)

Instructions:

1. **Season the Steaks:**
   - Pat the steaks dry and season generously with salt and pepper on both sides.
2. **Sear the Steaks:**
   - Heat olive oil in a skillet over high heat. Add steaks and sear for about 3-4 minutes per side for medium-rare, or longer to reach desired doneness.
3. **Add Flavor:**
   - Reduce heat to medium. Add garlic and butter to the skillet. Spoon melted butter over the steaks as they cook for added flavor.
4. **Rest and Serve:**
   - Remove steaks from the skillet and let rest for 5 minutes. Garnish with fresh rosemary or thyme if desired.

Enjoy your perfectly cooked Filet Mignon!

Eggplant Parmesan

Ingredients:

For the Eggplant:

- 2 large eggplants, sliced into 1/4-inch rounds
- Salt, for sprinkling
- 1 cup all-purpose flour
- 3 large eggs, beaten
- 2 cups breadcrumbs
- 1 cup grated Parmesan cheese

For the Sauce:

- 2 cups marinara sauce
- 1 cup shredded mozzarella cheese
- 1/4 cup chopped fresh basil (optional)
- 1/4 cup olive oil (for frying)

Instructions:

1. **Prepare the Eggplant:**
    - Preheat your oven to 375°F (190°C).
    - Sprinkle eggplant slices with salt and let sit for 30 minutes to draw out moisture. Rinse and pat dry with paper towels.
2. **Bread the Eggplant:**
    - Set up a breading station: one plate with flour, one with beaten eggs, and one with breadcrumbs mixed with grated Parmesan cheese.
    - Dredge each eggplant slice in flour, then dip in eggs, and coat with the breadcrumb mixture.
3. **Fry the Eggplant:**
    - Heat olive oil in a large skillet over medium heat. Fry eggplant slices in batches until golden brown and crispy, about 2-3 minutes per side. Drain on paper towels.
4. **Assemble the Dish:**
    - In a baking dish, spread a thin layer of marinara sauce. Arrange a layer of fried eggplant slices over the sauce. Spread some marinara sauce on top of the eggplant, then sprinkle with mozzarella cheese. Repeat layers until all ingredients are used, finishing with a layer of sauce and cheese.
5. **Bake:**
    - Bake in the preheated oven for 25-30 minutes, or until the cheese is melted and bubbly and the sauce is hot.
6. **Garnish and Serve:**
    - Garnish with fresh basil if desired. Let cool slightly before serving.

Enjoy your homemade Eggplant Parmesan!

Thai Green Curry

Ingredients:

- 1 tbsp vegetable oil
- 2-3 tbsp green curry paste (adjust to taste)
- 1 can (14 oz) coconut milk
- 1 cup chicken or vegetable broth
- 1 lb (450 g) chicken breast or thigh, sliced
- 1 cup bamboo shoots (canned or fresh)
- 1 red bell pepper, sliced
- 1 cup snap peas or green beans
- 1 tbsp fish sauce (or soy sauce for a vegetarian option)
- 1 tbsp brown sugar
- 1/2 cup fresh basil leaves
- Cooked jasmine rice, for serving

Instructions:

1. **Cook the Curry Paste:**
    - Heat oil in a large skillet or wok over medium heat. Add green curry paste and cook, stirring, for about 1-2 minutes until fragrant.
2. **Add Liquids:**
    - Pour in coconut milk and broth, stirring to combine. Bring to a simmer.
3. **Cook the Chicken:**
    - Add sliced chicken to the skillet. Simmer for about 5-7 minutes, or until the chicken is cooked through.
4. **Add Vegetables:**
    - Stir in bamboo shoots, red bell pepper, and snap peas. Cook for an additional 5 minutes, or until vegetables are tender.
5. **Season and Finish:**
    - Stir in fish sauce and brown sugar. Adjust seasoning as needed.
6. **Serve:**
    - Garnish with fresh basil leaves. Serve over jasmine rice.

Enjoy your flavorful Thai Green Curry!

BBQ Ribs

Ingredients:

- 2 racks of baby back ribs
- 1/4 cup brown sugar
- 1 tbsp smoked paprika
- 1 tbsp chili powder
- 1 tsp garlic powder
- 1 tsp onion powder
- 1/2 tsp cumin
- 1/2 tsp black pepper
- 1/2 tsp salt
- 1 cup BBQ sauce

Instructions:

1. **Prepare the Ribs:**
    - Preheat your oven to 300°F (150°C).
    - Remove the membrane from the back of the ribs if it's still attached.
2. **Season the Ribs:**
    - Mix brown sugar, smoked paprika, chili powder, garlic powder, onion powder, cumin, black pepper, and salt in a bowl.
    - Rub the spice mixture evenly over both sides of the ribs.
3. **Bake:**
    - Place ribs on a baking sheet lined with foil and cover with another layer of foil.
    - Bake for 2.5 to 3 hours, or until the ribs are tender.
4. **Grill (Optional for Extra Flavor):**
    - Preheat your grill to medium-high heat.
    - Brush the cooked ribs with BBQ sauce and grill for 5-10 minutes, turning occasionally, until caramelized.
5. **Serve:**
    - Let the ribs rest for a few minutes before cutting. Serve with additional BBQ sauce on the side.

Enjoy your tender and flavorful BBQ Ribs!

Beef Stroganoff

Ingredients:

- 1 lb (450 g) beef sirloin or tenderloin, cut into thin strips
- Salt and freshly ground black pepper, to taste
- 2 tbsp olive oil or butter
- 1 medium onion, finely chopped
- 2 cloves garlic, minced
- 8 oz (225 g) mushrooms, sliced
- 1 cup beef broth
- 1 cup sour cream
- 1 tbsp Dijon mustard
- 1 tbsp all-purpose flour (optional, for thickening)
- Fresh parsley, chopped (for garnish)
- Cooked egg noodles or rice, for serving

Instructions:

1. **Prepare the Beef:**
   - Season beef strips with salt and pepper.
   - Heat olive oil or butter in a large skillet over medium-high heat. Add beef strips in batches, cooking until browned on all sides. Remove beef and set aside.
2. **Cook the Vegetables:**
   - In the same skillet, add a bit more oil if needed. Sauté onion until soft, about 3-4 minutes.
   - Add garlic and cook for another 30 seconds.
   - Add mushrooms and cook until browned and tender, about 5-7 minutes.
3. **Make the Sauce:**
   - Stir in flour if using and cook for 1 minute.
   - Add beef broth, stirring to combine. Bring to a simmer and cook until slightly reduced, about 5 minutes.
   - Lower the heat and stir in sour cream and Dijon mustard. Cook until heated through.
4. **Combine:**
   - Return the cooked beef along with any accumulated juices to the skillet. Stir to coat the beef in the sauce and heat through, about 2-3 minutes.
5. **Serve:**
   - Garnish with fresh parsley. Serve over cooked egg noodles or rice.

Enjoy your creamy and flavorful Beef Stroganoff!

Chicken Tikka Masala

Ingredients:

For the Marinade:

- 1 lb (450 g) chicken breast or thighs, cut into bite-sized pieces
- 1 cup plain yogurt
- 2 tbsp lemon juice
- 1 tbsp ground cumin
- 1 tbsp ground coriander
- 1 tsp paprika
- 1 tsp turmeric
- 1/2 tsp ground cinnamon
- 1/2 tsp cayenne pepper (optional, for heat)
- Salt, to taste

For the Sauce:

- 2 tbsp vegetable oil
- 1 large onion, finely chopped
- 3 cloves garlic, minced
- 1 tbsp ginger, minced
- 1 can (14 oz) crushed tomatoes
- 1 cup heavy cream
- 1 tbsp ground cumin
- 1 tbsp ground coriander
- 1 tsp paprika
- 1 tsp garam masala
- 1/2 tsp turmeric
- Salt and pepper, to taste
- Fresh cilantro, chopped (for garnish)

Instructions:

1. **Marinate the Chicken:**
   - Combine yogurt, lemon juice, cumin, coriander, paprika, turmeric, cinnamon, cayenne pepper, and salt in a bowl. Add chicken and coat well. Marinate in the fridge for at least 1 hour or overnight.
2. **Cook the Chicken:**
   - Preheat grill or broiler. Thread chicken pieces onto skewers or place on a baking sheet.
   - Grill or broil for 5-7 minutes per side, or until cooked through and slightly charred. Set aside.

3. **Prepare the Sauce:**
    - Heat oil in a large skillet over medium heat. Sauté onion until soft, about 5 minutes.
    - Add garlic and ginger; cook for 1 minute.
    - Stir in crushed tomatoes, cream, cumin, coriander, paprika, garam masala, and turmeric. Simmer for 10 minutes, stirring occasionally.
4. **Combine and Serve:**
    - Add cooked chicken to the sauce. Simmer for another 5 minutes to blend flavors.
    - Garnish with chopped cilantro. Serve with rice or naan.

Enjoy your flavorful Chicken Tikka Masala!

Clam Chowder

Ingredients:

- 4 slices bacon, chopped
- 1 onion, finely chopped
- 2 celery stalks, diced
- 2 cloves garlic, minced
- 2 tbsp all-purpose flour
- 2 cups clam juice
- 1 cup chicken broth
- 2 cups potatoes, peeled and diced
- 1 cup heavy cream
- 1 can (6.5 oz) chopped clams, drained and reserved
- 1 tsp dried thyme
- Salt and freshly ground black pepper, to taste
- Fresh parsley, chopped (for garnish)

Instructions:

1. **Cook the Bacon:**
    - In a large pot, cook bacon over medium heat until crispy. Remove bacon and set aside, leaving the drippings in the pot.
2. **Sauté Vegetables:**
    - Add onion and celery to the pot and cook until softened, about 5 minutes.
    - Stir in garlic and cook for 1 minute.
3. **Make the Base:**
    - Sprinkle flour over the vegetables and stir to combine. Cook for 1-2 minutes.
    - Gradually add clam juice and chicken broth, stirring constantly to avoid lumps.
4. **Cook the Potatoes:**
    - Add diced potatoes and thyme. Bring to a boil, then reduce heat and simmer until potatoes are tender, about 10-15 minutes.
5. **Add Cream and Clams:**
    - Stir in heavy cream and reserved clams. Heat through but do not boil. Season with salt and pepper to taste.
6. **Serve:**
    - Garnish with crispy bacon and fresh parsley. Serve hot with oyster crackers or crusty bread.

Enjoy your creamy and comforting Clam Chowder!

Pad Thai

Ingredients:

- 8 oz (225 g) rice noodles
- 2 tbsp vegetable oil
- 1/2 cup diced tofu or chicken (optional)
- 2 cloves garlic, minced
- 1/2 cup bean sprouts
- 1/2 cup shredded carrots
- 2 green onions, chopped
- 2 large eggs, lightly beaten
- 1/4 cup chopped peanuts
- Fresh cilantro, chopped (for garnish)
- Lime wedges (for serving)

For the Sauce:

- 1/4 cup fish sauce (or soy sauce for a vegetarian option)
- 1/4 cup tamarind paste
- 3 tbsp brown sugar
- 1 tbsp soy sauce
- 1/2 tsp red pepper flakes (optional, for heat)

Instructions:

1. **Prepare the Noodles:**
    - Cook rice noodles according to package instructions. Drain and set aside.
2. **Make the Sauce:**
    - In a small bowl, mix together fish sauce, tamarind paste, brown sugar, soy sauce, and red pepper flakes. Stir until sugar is dissolved and set aside.
3. **Cook the Protein:**
    - Heat oil in a large skillet or wok over medium-high heat. Add tofu or chicken (if using) and cook until browned and cooked through. Remove from skillet and set aside.
4. **Stir-Fry Vegetables:**
    - In the same skillet, add garlic and cook for 30 seconds until fragrant.
    - Add bean sprouts and shredded carrots. Stir-fry for 2-3 minutes.
5. **Add Noodles and Eggs:**
    - Push vegetables to one side of the skillet. Pour beaten eggs into the empty side and scramble until just set.
    - Add cooked noodles and sauce to the skillet. Toss everything together until well combined and heated through.
6. **Finish and Serve:**

- Stir in cooked tofu or chicken and green onions.
- Garnish with chopped peanuts and fresh cilantro.
- Serve with lime wedges on the side.

Enjoy your flavorful Pad Thai!

Beef Tacos

Ingredients:

- 1 lb (450 g) ground beef
- 1 small onion, finely chopped
- 2 cloves garlic, minced
- 1 tbsp chili powder
- 1 tsp ground cumin
- 1 tsp paprika
- 1/2 tsp dried oregano
- 1/2 tsp salt
- 1/4 tsp black pepper
- 1/2 cup beef broth
- 8 taco shells or tortillas
- Toppings: shredded lettuce, diced tomatoes, shredded cheese, sour cream, salsa, chopped cilantro (optional)

Instructions:

1. **Cook the Beef:**
   - In a large skillet over medium heat, cook ground beef until browned. Drain excess fat.
2. **Add Vegetables and Seasoning:**
   - Add onion and garlic to the skillet. Cook until onion is soft, about 5 minutes.
   - Stir in chili powder, cumin, paprika, oregano, salt, and pepper. Cook for 1 minute.
3. **Simmer:**
   - Add beef broth. Stir and simmer until the mixture thickens slightly, about 5-7 minutes.
4. **Prepare the Tacos:**
   - Warm taco shells or tortillas according to package instructions.
5. **Assemble:**
   - Spoon beef mixture into taco shells or tortillas. Top with your choice of shredded lettuce, diced tomatoes, shredded cheese, sour cream, salsa, and chopped cilantro.

Enjoy your tasty Beef Tacos!

Mushroom Risotto

Ingredients:

- 1 cup Arborio rice
- 4 cups chicken or vegetable broth
- 1 cup white wine (optional, can substitute with extra broth)
- 2 tbsp olive oil
- 1 small onion, finely chopped
- 2 cloves garlic, minced
- 2 cups mushrooms (such as cremini or button), sliced
- 1/2 cup grated Parmesan cheese
- 2 tbsp unsalted butter
- Salt and freshly ground black pepper, to taste
- Fresh parsley, chopped (for garnish)

Instructions:

1. **Prepare the Broth:**
   - In a saucepan, keep the broth warm over low heat.
2. **Cook the Mushrooms:**
   - In a large skillet or saucepan, heat olive oil over medium heat. Add mushrooms and cook until browned and tender, about 5-7 minutes. Remove from skillet and set aside.
3. **Sauté Onion and Garlic:**
   - In the same skillet, add a bit more olive oil if needed. Sauté onion until translucent, about 3-4 minutes. Add garlic and cook for another 30 seconds.
4. **Add Rice:**
   - Stir in Arborio rice and cook, stirring frequently, for about 2 minutes until the rice is lightly toasted and coated with the oil.
5. **Deglaze with Wine:**
   - Pour in white wine (if using) and cook, stirring, until the wine is mostly absorbed.
6. **Add Broth Gradually:**
   - Begin adding the warm broth, one ladleful at a time, stirring constantly and allowing each addition to be absorbed before adding the next. Continue until the rice is creamy and al dente, about 18-20 minutes.
7. **Finish the Risotto:**
   - Stir in the cooked mushrooms, Parmesan cheese, and butter. Season with salt and pepper to taste. Cook for an additional 1-2 minutes until everything is well combined and heated through.
8. **Serve:**
   - Garnish with fresh parsley if desired. Serve immediately.

Enjoy your rich and creamy Mushroom Risotto!

Salmon Teriyaki

Ingredients:

- 4 salmon fillets (6 oz each)
- 1/4 cup soy sauce
- 1/4 cup mirin (Japanese sweet rice wine)
- 2 tbsp honey or brown sugar
- 2 tbsp rice vinegar
- 2 cloves garlic, minced
- 1 tsp fresh ginger, minced
- 1 tbsp cornstarch (optional, for thickening)
- 1 tbsp water (if using cornstarch)
- 1 tbsp vegetable oil
- Sesame seeds and chopped green onions (for garnish)

Instructions:

1. **Prepare the Marinade:**
    - In a small bowl, mix together soy sauce, mirin, honey (or brown sugar), rice vinegar, garlic, and ginger.
2. **Marinate the Salmon:**
    - Place salmon fillets in a shallow dish or resealable plastic bag. Pour half of the marinade over the salmon, ensuring they are well coated. Marinate in the refrigerator for at least 30 minutes, up to 2 hours.
3. **Cook the Salmon:**
    - Preheat your oven to 400°F (200°C) or heat a grill to medium-high heat.
    - If baking, line a baking sheet with parchment paper or lightly oil it. Place salmon fillets skin-side down on the sheet. Bake for 12-15 minutes, or until salmon is cooked through and flakes easily with a fork.
    - If grilling, brush the grill grates with oil and place the salmon fillets on the grill. Cook for about 4-5 minutes per side, or until the salmon is cooked through.
4. **Make the Teriyaki Sauce (Optional Thickening):**
    - While the salmon is cooking, pour the remaining marinade into a small saucepan. Bring to a simmer over medium heat.
    - If you prefer a thicker sauce, mix cornstarch with water and add to the saucepan. Stir until the sauce thickens, about 1-2 minutes. Remove from heat.
5. **Serve:**
    - Drizzle the teriyaki sauce over the cooked salmon. Garnish with sesame seeds and chopped green onions.

Enjoy your flavorful and savory Salmon Teriyaki!

Lasagna

Ingredients:

For the Meat Sauce:

- 1 lb (450 g) ground beef
- 1 onion, chopped
- 2 cloves garlic, minced
- 1 can (14 oz) crushed tomatoes
- 1 can (6 oz) tomato paste
- 1/2 cup tomato sauce
- 2 tbsp olive oil
- 1 tsp dried basil
- 1 tsp dried oregano
- Salt and pepper, to taste

For the Cheese Mixture:

- 1 container (15 oz) ricotta cheese
- 1 cup grated Parmesan cheese
- 1 large egg
- 2 cups shredded mozzarella cheese
- 2 tbsp chopped fresh parsley (optional)

For Assembly:

- 12 lasagna noodles
- Extra shredded mozzarella cheese (for topping)

Instructions:

1. **Cook the Meat Sauce:**
    - Heat olive oil in a large skillet over medium heat. Add onion and garlic, cooking until softened.
    - Add ground beef and cook until browned. Drain excess fat.
    - Stir in crushed tomatoes, tomato paste, tomato sauce, basil, oregano, salt, and pepper. Simmer for 20-30 minutes, stirring occasionally.
2. **Prepare the Cheese Mixture:**
    - In a bowl, mix ricotta cheese, Parmesan cheese, egg, and parsley (if using). Set aside.
3. **Cook the Noodles:**
    - Cook lasagna noodles according to package instructions. Drain and lay out on a sheet of parchment paper or foil to prevent sticking.
4. **Assemble the Lasagna:**

    - Preheat oven to 375°F (190°C).
    - Spread a thin layer of meat sauce on the bottom of a 9x13-inch baking dish.
    - Place a layer of noodles over the sauce. Spread a layer of the cheese mixture over the noodles, followed by a layer of meat sauce. Repeat layers, ending with a layer of meat sauce.
    - Sprinkle extra mozzarella cheese on top.
5. **Bake:**
    - Cover with foil and bake for 25 minutes. Remove foil and bake for an additional 20 minutes, or until cheese is melted and bubbly.
6. **Cool and Serve:**
    - Let the lasagna rest for 10-15 minutes before cutting and serving.

Enjoy your hearty and delicious Lasagna!

Chicken Marsala

Ingredients:

- 4 boneless, skinless chicken breasts (about 1.5 lbs total)
- Salt and freshly ground black pepper, to taste
- 1/2 cup all-purpose flour
- 2 tbsp olive oil
- 4 tbsp unsalted butter, divided
- 1 cup mushrooms, sliced (cremini or button mushrooms work well)
- 3/4 cup Marsala wine (dry or sweet, depending on preference)
- 1 cup chicken broth
- 2 cloves garlic, minced
- 1 tbsp fresh parsley, chopped (for garnish)

Instructions:

1. **Prepare the Chicken:**
   - Place chicken breasts between two sheets of plastic wrap or parchment paper. Pound to an even thickness, about 1/2 inch thick.
   - Season both sides with salt and pepper.
   - Dredge each chicken breast in flour, shaking off excess.
2. **Cook the Chicken:**
   - Heat olive oil in a large skillet over medium-high heat. Add 2 tablespoons of butter.
   - Once the butter has melted and the skillet is hot, add chicken breasts. Cook until golden brown and cooked through, about 4-5 minutes per side. Remove chicken from skillet and set aside.
3. **Cook the Mushrooms:**
   - In the same skillet, add the remaining 2 tablespoons of butter. Add mushrooms and cook until tender and browned, about 5 minutes.
   - Add garlic and cook for another 1 minute.
4. **Make the Sauce:**
   - Pour Marsala wine into the skillet, scraping up any browned bits from the bottom of the pan. Simmer for 2-3 minutes until the wine is slightly reduced.
   - Add chicken broth and simmer for another 5 minutes, or until the sauce is reduced and slightly thickened.
5. **Combine and Serve:**
   - Return the chicken breasts to the skillet and coat with the sauce. Simmer for 2-3 minutes to heat through.
   - Garnish with chopped parsley.

Serve Chicken Marsala with mashed potatoes, pasta, or rice to soak up the delicious sauce. Enjoy!

Greek Salad

Ingredients:

- 1 large cucumber, peeled and chopped
- 2-3 ripe tomatoes, chopped
- 1/2 red onion, thinly sliced
- 1/2 cup Kalamata olives, pitted
- 1/2 cup feta cheese, crumbled or in large chunks
- 1/4 cup extra virgin olive oil
- 2 tbsp red wine vinegar
- 1 tsp dried oregano
- Salt and freshly ground black pepper, to taste
- Fresh parsley or basil, chopped (optional, for garnish)

Instructions:

1. **Prepare the Vegetables:**
   - In a large bowl, combine chopped cucumber, tomatoes, red onion, and Kalamata olives.
2. **Add the Cheese:**
   - Gently fold in the feta cheese.
3. **Make the Dressing:**
   - In a small bowl or jar, whisk together olive oil, red wine vinegar, oregano, salt, and pepper.
4. **Dress the Salad:**
   - Pour the dressing over the salad and toss gently to combine.
5. **Garnish and Serve:**
   - Garnish with fresh parsley or basil if desired. Serve immediately or chill in the refrigerator for 30 minutes to allow flavors to meld.

Enjoy your vibrant and tangy Greek Salad!

Peking Duck

Ingredients:

- 1 whole duck (about 5-6 lbs)
- 2 tbsp soy sauce
- 1 tbsp hoisin sauce
- 1 tbsp honey
- 1 tbsp rice vinegar
- 1/2 tsp five-spice powder
- 1/2 cup water
- 2-3 green onions, sliced (for garnish)
- Chinese pancakes or tortillas (for serving)
- Cucumber slices (for garnish)
- Additional hoisin sauce (for serving)

Instructions:

1. **Prepare the Duck:**
    - Preheat oven to 375°F (190°C).
    - Rinse the duck and pat dry. Remove excess fat from the cavity and trim any extra skin.
2. **Season the Duck:**
    - Mix soy sauce, hoisin sauce, honey, rice vinegar, five-spice powder, and water in a bowl.
    - Brush the mixture all over the duck, including inside the cavity.
3. **Roast the Duck:**
    - Place the duck on a rack in a roasting pan. Roast for about 1.5 to 2 hours, or until the skin is crispy and the meat is fully cooked, basting occasionally with the pan juices.
4. **Serve:**
    - Let the duck rest for 10 minutes before carving. Slice thinly.
    - Serve with Chinese pancakes or tortillas, hoisin sauce, sliced cucumber, and green onions.

Enjoy your crispy and flavorful Peking Duck!

Shrimp and Grits

Ingredients:

For the Grits:

- 1 cup stone-ground grits
- 4 cups water or chicken broth
- 1 cup milk or cream
- 2 tbsp butter
- 1 cup shredded cheddar cheese (optional)
- Salt and black pepper, to taste

For the Shrimp:

- 1 lb (450 g) large shrimp, peeled and deveined
- 4 slices bacon, chopped
- 1 red bell pepper, diced
- 1 green bell pepper, diced
- 1 small onion, finely chopped
- 3 cloves garlic, minced
- 1/2 cup chicken broth
- 1 tbsp Worcestershire sauce
- 1 tbsp lemon juice
- 1 tsp smoked paprika
- 1/2 tsp cayenne pepper (optional, for heat)
- Salt and black pepper, to taste
- 2 tbsp chopped fresh parsley (for garnish)

Instructions:

1. Cook the Grits:

- In a medium pot, bring water or chicken broth to a boil. Gradually whisk in grits.
- Reduce heat to low, cover, and cook, stirring occasionally, for 20-25 minutes, or until grits are tender and thickened.
- Stir in milk or cream, butter, and cheddar cheese (if using). Season with salt and pepper to taste. Keep warm.

2. Prepare the Shrimp:

- In a large skillet over medium heat, cook chopped bacon until crispy. Remove bacon and drain on paper towels, leaving the bacon drippings in the skillet.

- Add diced bell peppers, onion, and garlic to the skillet. Cook until vegetables are softened, about 5 minutes.
- Add shrimp to the skillet and cook for 3-4 minutes per side, or until shrimp are pink and opaque.
- Stir in chicken broth, Worcestershire sauce, lemon juice, smoked paprika, cayenne pepper (if using), salt, and pepper. Cook for 2 minutes, allowing the sauce to reduce slightly.

3. Assemble and Serve:

- Spoon grits onto plates or bowls. Top with shrimp mixture.
- Garnish with crispy bacon and chopped parsley.

Enjoy your creamy, savory Shrimp and Grits!

Teriyaki Chicken

Ingredients:

For the Marinade/Sauce:

- 1/2 cup soy sauce
- 1/4 cup mirin (or white wine)
- 1/4 cup brown sugar
- 2 tbsp rice vinegar
- 2 cloves garlic, minced
- 1 tsp fresh ginger, minced
- 1 tbsp cornstarch (optional, for thickening)
- 1 tbsp water (if using cornstarch)

For the Chicken:

- 4 boneless, skinless chicken thighs or breasts
- 1 tbsp vegetable oil
- Sesame seeds (for garnish)
- Chopped green onions (for garnish)

Instructions:

1. **Prepare the Marinade/Sauce:**
    - In a bowl, whisk together soy sauce, mirin, brown sugar, rice vinegar, garlic, and ginger.
    - If you prefer a thicker sauce, mix cornstarch with water and stir into the marinade.
2. **Marinate the Chicken:**
    - Place chicken in a resealable plastic bag or shallow dish. Pour half of the marinade over the chicken, ensuring it's well-coated. Marinate in the refrigerator for at least 30 minutes or up to 2 hours.
3. **Cook the Chicken:**
    - Heat vegetable oil in a large skillet over medium-high heat. Remove chicken from marinade and cook in the skillet for 6-7 minutes per side, or until cooked through and internal temperature reaches 165°F (74°C). Discard the marinade used for marinating.
    - In the last few minutes of cooking, pour the remaining marinade over the chicken. Let it simmer and thicken slightly if using cornstarch.
4. **Serve:**
    - Slice the chicken and serve over rice or with steamed vegetables.
    - Garnish with sesame seeds and chopped green onions.

Enjoy your flavorful Teriyaki Chicken!

Butternut Squash Soup

Ingredients:

- **1 medium butternut squash** (about 2 lbs), peeled, seeded, and cubed
- **2 tbsp olive oil**
- **1 large onion**, chopped
- **2 cloves garlic**, minced
- **1 large carrot**, peeled and chopped
- **1 celery stalk**, chopped
- **4 cups vegetable or chicken broth**
- **1/2 cup coconut milk** or heavy cream (for a creamier texture)
- **1/2 tsp ground ginger** (optional)
- **1/2 tsp ground cumin** (optional)
- **Salt and freshly ground black pepper**, to taste
- **Fresh thyme** or **sage**, for garnish
- **Croutons**, for garnish (optional)

Instructions:

1. **Prepare the Butternut Squash:**
    - Preheat your oven to 400°F (200°C).
    - Peel, seed, and cube the butternut squash. Toss the cubes with 1 tablespoon of olive oil and a pinch of salt and pepper.
    - Spread the squash cubes on a baking sheet in a single layer. Roast for 25-30 minutes, or until tender and lightly caramelized, stirring halfway through.
2. **Cook the Vegetables:**
    - While the squash is roasting, heat the remaining 1 tablespoon of olive oil in a large pot over medium heat.
    - Add the chopped onion, carrot, and celery. Sauté for 8-10 minutes, or until the vegetables are softened and the onion is translucent.
    - Add the minced garlic and cook for an additional 1-2 minutes, until fragrant.
3. **Combine and Simmer:**
    - Once the squash is roasted, add it to the pot with the sautéed vegetables.
    - Pour in the vegetable or chicken broth and bring to a simmer. Cook for 10-15 minutes, allowing the flavors to meld.
4. **Blend the Soup:**
    - Use an immersion blender to puree the soup directly in the pot until smooth. Alternatively, carefully transfer the soup in batches to a blender and blend until smooth. Return the blended soup to the pot if using a blender.
5. **Finish and Season:**
    - Stir in the coconut milk or heavy cream. If using, add ground ginger and cumin. Season with salt and pepper to taste.

- Simmer for an additional 5 minutes to heat through and combine flavors.
6. **Serve:**
    - Ladle the soup into bowls. Garnish with fresh thyme or sage and croutons if desired.

Enjoy your delicious and creamy Butternut Squash Soup!

Beef Bourguignon

Ingredients:

- **2 lbs (900 g) beef chuck**, cut into 1.5-inch cubes
- **Salt and freshly ground black pepper**, to taste
- **3 tbsp all-purpose flour**
- **4 tbsp vegetable oil**, divided
- **1 medium onion**, chopped
- **2 carrots**, peeled and sliced
- **2 cloves garlic**, minced
- **1 cup red wine** (Burgundy or Pinot Noir)
- **2 cups beef broth**
- **2 tbsp tomato paste**
- **1 tsp dried thyme**
- **1 bay leaf**
- **1 cup pearl onions** (or small onions, peeled)
- **1 cup mushrooms**, sliced
- **4 oz (115 g) bacon**, chopped
- **2 tbsp unsalted butter**
- **Fresh parsley**, chopped (for garnish)

Instructions:

1. **Prepare the Beef:**
    - Preheat your oven to 350°F (175°C).
    - Season the beef cubes with salt and pepper. Dust with flour, shaking off excess.
2. **Brown the Beef:**
    - Heat 2 tablespoons of vegetable oil in a large Dutch oven or heavy pot over medium-high heat. Brown the beef in batches, adding more oil as needed. Remove beef and set aside.
3. **Sauté Vegetables:**
    - In the same pot, add the remaining 2 tablespoons of oil. Sauté onion and carrots until softened, about 5 minutes.
    - Add garlic and cook for another minute.
4. **Deglaze and Simmer:**
    - Return the beef to the pot. Stir in tomato paste and cook for 2 minutes.
    - Pour in the red wine, scraping up any browned bits from the bottom of the pot. Bring to a simmer and cook for 5 minutes.
    - Add beef broth, thyme, and bay leaf. Bring to a boil.
5. **Cook in Oven:**
    - Cover the pot and transfer it to the preheated oven. Bake for 2 to 2.5 hours, or until the beef is tender.

6. **Prepare the Garnishes:**
    - While the beef is cooking, heat butter in a skillet over medium heat. Cook the bacon until crispy. Remove bacon and set aside.
    - In the same skillet, cook pearl onions and mushrooms until browned and tender. Set aside.
7. **Finish the Dish:**
    - After the beef has finished cooking, stir in the cooked bacon, pearl onions, and mushrooms.
    - Return the pot to the oven, uncovered, for an additional 30 minutes to meld flavors.
8. **Serve:**
    - Garnish with chopped parsley. Serve over mashed potatoes, rice, or with crusty bread.

Enjoy your delicious Beef Bourguignon!

Chicken Enchiladas

Ingredients:

For the Filling:

- **2 cups cooked chicken**, shredded (use rotisserie or poached)
- **1 cup shredded cheddar cheese** (or a blend of cheeses)
- **1 cup sour cream**
- **1 cup enchilada sauce** (store-bought or homemade)
- **1 small onion**, finely chopped
- **1 can (4 oz) diced green chilies** (optional, for added flavor)
- **1 tsp ground cumin**
- **1/2 tsp garlic powder**
- **Salt and black pepper**, to taste

For Assembly:

- **8-10 small flour or corn tortillas**
- **2 cups enchilada sauce** (for topping)
- **1 cup shredded cheese** (for topping)
- **Chopped fresh cilantro** (for garnish, optional)
- **Sour cream** (for serving)

Instructions:

1. **Prepare the Filling:**
   - In a large bowl, mix shredded chicken, shredded cheese, sour cream, 1 cup enchilada sauce, onion, green chilies (if using), cumin, garlic powder, salt, and pepper.
2. **Preheat Oven:**
   - Preheat your oven to 375°F (190°C).
3. **Assemble Enchiladas:**
   - Warm the tortillas slightly to make them easier to roll (either in the microwave or in a hot skillet).
   - Spoon about 1/4 cup of the chicken mixture onto each tortilla. Roll up and place seam-side down in a greased baking dish.
4. **Add Sauce and Cheese:**
   - Pour the remaining 2 cups of enchilada sauce over the rolled tortillas.
   - Sprinkle the top with 1 cup of shredded cheese.
5. **Bake:**
   - Cover with foil and bake for 20 minutes. Remove the foil and bake for an additional 10-15 minutes, or until the cheese is melted and bubbly.
6. **Garnish and Serve:**
   - Garnish with chopped cilantro if desired. Serve with extra sour cream on the side.

Enjoy your delicious Chicken Enchiladas!

Vegetable Tempura

Ingredients:

For the Tempura Batter:

- **1 cup all-purpose flour**
- **1/2 cup cornstarch**
- **1 tsp baking powder**
- **1 cup ice-cold sparkling water** (or very cold water)
- **1 egg**, lightly beaten

For the Vegetables:

- **1 cup sweet potato**, peeled and sliced into thin rounds
- **1 cup zucchini**, sliced into thin rounds
- **1 cup bell pepper**, sliced into strips
- **1 cup mushrooms**, sliced
- **1 cup broccoli florets**

For Frying:

- **Vegetable oil** (for deep frying)

For Dipping Sauce (Tentsuyu):

- **1/2 cup dashi** (or chicken/vegetable broth)
- **1/4 cup soy sauce**
- **1/4 cup mirin** (or white wine)
- **1 tbsp sugar** (optional)

Instructions:

1. **Prepare the Batter:**
    - In a bowl, whisk together flour, cornstarch, and baking powder.
    - In a separate bowl, mix ice-cold sparkling water and beaten egg.
    - Gently fold the wet ingredients into the dry ingredients. The batter should be lumpy; do not overmix.
2. **Prepare the Vegetables:**
    - Slice and prepare the vegetables as described. Pat them dry with paper towels to remove excess moisture.
3. **Heat the Oil:**
    - Heat vegetable oil in a deep pan or fryer to 350°F (175°C). The oil should be enough to fully submerge the vegetables.

4. **Fry the Vegetables:**
    - Dip vegetables into the tempura batter, allowing excess batter to drip off.
    - Carefully place the battered vegetables into the hot oil, frying in batches to avoid overcrowding. Fry until golden and crispy, about 2-3 minutes per batch.
    - Remove with a slotted spoon and drain on paper towels.
5. **Prepare the Dipping Sauce:**
    - In a small saucepan, combine dashi, soy sauce, mirin, and sugar (if using). Bring to a simmer over medium heat. Remove from heat and let cool slightly.
6. **Serve:**
    - Serve the vegetable tempura hot with dipping sauce on the side.

Enjoy your crispy and delicious Vegetable Tempura!

Lobster Mac and Cheese

Ingredients:

For the Mac and Cheese:

- **8 oz (225 g) elbow macaroni** or other pasta
- **2 cups lobster meat**, cooked and chopped (fresh or thawed from frozen)
- **2 cups shredded sharp cheddar cheese**
- **1 cup shredded Gruyère cheese**
- **2 tbsp unsalted butter**
- **2 tbsp all-purpose flour**
- **1 1/2 cups whole milk**
- **1/2 cup heavy cream**
- **1/2 tsp garlic powder**
- **1/2 tsp onion powder**
- **1/4 tsp paprika**
- **Salt and freshly ground black pepper**, to taste

For the Topping:

- **1/2 cup panko breadcrumbs**
- **1/4 cup grated Parmesan cheese**
- **1 tbsp unsalted butter**, melted
- **2 tbsp chopped fresh parsley** (optional, for garnish)

Instructions:

1. **Cook the Pasta:**
   - Cook macaroni according to package instructions until al dente. Drain and set aside.
2. **Prepare the Cheese Sauce:**
   - In a large saucepan, melt 2 tablespoons of butter over medium heat.
   - Stir in flour and cook for 1-2 minutes, until it forms a smooth paste (roux).
   - Gradually whisk in the milk and heavy cream, ensuring there are no lumps. Continue to cook, stirring constantly, until the sauce thickens, about 5-7 minutes.
   - Reduce heat to low and stir in the cheddar and Gruyère cheeses until melted and smooth. Season with garlic powder, onion powder, paprika, salt, and pepper.
3. **Combine Pasta and Lobster:**
   - Gently fold in the cooked macaroni and lobster meat into the cheese sauce until well combined.
4. **Prepare the Topping:**
   - In a small bowl, mix panko breadcrumbs, Parmesan cheese, and melted butter.
5. **Assemble and Bake:**

    - Preheat your oven to 375°F (190°C).
    - Transfer the macaroni and cheese mixture to a greased baking dish.
    - Sprinkle the breadcrumb topping evenly over the macaroni and cheese.
    - Bake for 20-25 minutes, or until the top is golden and crispy and the cheese is bubbling.
6. **Garnish and Serve:**
    - Garnish with chopped fresh parsley if desired.

Enjoy your rich and creamy Lobster Mac and Cheese!

Coq au Vin

Ingredients:

- **4-6 chicken thighs** (bone-in, skin-on)
- **Salt and freshly ground black pepper**, to taste
- **2 tbsp vegetable oil**
- **4 slices bacon**, chopped
- **1 large onion**, chopped
- **2 carrots**, peeled and sliced
- **3 cloves garlic**, minced
- **2 tbsp all-purpose flour**
- **2 cups red wine** (such as Burgundy or Pinot Noir)
- **1 cup chicken broth**
- **2 tbsp tomato paste**
- **1 tbsp fresh thyme** (or 1 tsp dried thyme)
- **2 bay leaves**
- **1 cup pearl onions** (or small onions, peeled)
- **1 cup mushrooms**, sliced
- **2 tbsp unsalted butter**
- **Chopped fresh parsley** (for garnish)

Instructions:

1. **Prepare the Chicken:**
    - Season chicken thighs with salt and pepper.
    - In a large Dutch oven or heavy pot, heat vegetable oil over medium-high heat. Brown the chicken on all sides, about 5 minutes per side. Remove and set aside.
2. **Cook the Bacon and Vegetables:**
    - In the same pot, add chopped bacon and cook until crispy. Remove bacon and set aside, leaving the drippings in the pot.
    - Add onion and carrots to the pot. Sauté until softened, about 5-7 minutes.
    - Stir in garlic and cook for another minute.
3. **Make the Sauce:**
    - Sprinkle flour over the vegetables and cook for 1-2 minutes, stirring constantly.
    - Gradually pour in the red wine, scraping up any browned bits from the bottom of the pot. Stir in chicken broth and tomato paste.
    - Add thyme and bay leaves. Bring to a simmer.
4. **Simmer:**
    - Return the chicken and bacon to the pot. Cover and simmer on low heat for 30-40 minutes, or until the chicken is tender and cooked through.
5. **Cook the Garnishes:**

- While the chicken simmers, heat butter in a skillet over medium heat. Add pearl onions and mushrooms. Cook until browned and tender, about 10 minutes.
6. **Finish and Serve:**
    - Add the cooked pearl onions and mushrooms to the pot with the chicken. Simmer for an additional 5 minutes.
    - Discard bay leaves and thyme sprigs if used. Garnish with chopped fresh parsley.

Serve your Coq au Vin over mashed potatoes, noodles, or with crusty bread. Enjoy!

Pappardelle with Bolognese

Ingredients:

For the Bolognese Sauce:

- **2 tbsp olive oil**
- **1 medium onion**, finely chopped
- **2 carrots**, finely chopped
- **2 celery stalks**, finely chopped
- **4 cloves garlic**, minced
- **1 lb (450 g) ground beef**
- **1/2 lb (225 g) ground pork**
- **1 cup dry white wine** (or red wine)
- **1 cup whole milk**
- **1 can (14.5 oz) crushed tomatoes**
- **2 tbsp tomato paste**
- **1 tsp dried thyme**
- **1 tsp dried oregano**
- **1 bay leaf**
- **Salt and freshly ground black pepper**, to taste

For the Pappardelle:

- **12 oz (340 g) pappardelle pasta**
- **Salt**, for pasta water

For Garnish:

- **1/2 cup grated Parmesan cheese**
- **Fresh basil or parsley**, chopped (optional)

Instructions:

1. **Prepare the Bolognese Sauce:**
   - Heat olive oil in a large skillet or Dutch oven over medium heat.
   - Add the onion, carrots, and celery. Cook until softened, about 5-7 minutes.
   - Stir in garlic and cook for another 1-2 minutes.
   - Add the ground beef and pork. Cook, breaking up the meat with a spoon, until browned and cooked through, about 8-10 minutes.
   - Pour in the wine and let it simmer until mostly evaporated, about 5 minutes.
   - Stir in the milk, crushed tomatoes, tomato paste, thyme, oregano, and bay leaf. Bring to a simmer.

- Reduce heat to low, cover, and let simmer for 1.5 to 2 hours, stirring occasionally. Adjust seasoning with salt and pepper.
2. **Cook the Pappardelle:**
    - While the sauce is simmering, bring a large pot of salted water to a boil.
    - Cook the pappardelle according to package instructions until al dente. Reserve 1/2 cup of pasta water, then drain the pasta.
3. **Combine Pasta and Sauce:**
    - Add the cooked pappardelle to the Bolognese sauce. Toss gently to coat the pasta with the sauce. If needed, add a bit of the reserved pasta water to loosen the sauce.
4. **Serve:**
    - Divide the pappardelle with Bolognese among plates.
    - Garnish with grated Parmesan cheese and chopped basil or parsley if desired.

Enjoy your rich and comforting Pappardelle with Bolognese!

Moroccan Lamb Tagine

Ingredients:

- **2 lbs (900 g) lamb shoulder**, cut into chunks
- **2 tbsp olive oil**
- **1 large onion**, chopped
- **3 cloves garlic**, minced
- **1 tbsp ground cumin**
- **1 tbsp ground coriander**
- **1 tbsp ground paprika**
- **1 tsp ground cinnamon**
- **1/2 tsp ground ginger**
- **1/4 tsp ground turmeric**
- **1/2 tsp cayenne pepper** (optional, for heat)
- **1 can (14.5 oz) diced tomatoes**
- **1 cup chicken or beef broth**
- **1/2 cup dried apricots**, chopped
- **1/2 cup almonds**, toasted and roughly chopped
- **1/2 cup green olives**, pitted and sliced
- **1 tbsp honey**
- **Salt and freshly ground black pepper**, to taste
- **Fresh cilantro** or **parsley**, for garnish

For Serving:

- **Couscous** or **rice**

Instructions:

1. **Brown the Lamb:**
    - Heat olive oil in a large pot or tagine over medium-high heat.
    - Season lamb chunks with salt and pepper. Brown the lamb in batches, removing and setting aside each batch as it's browned.
2. **Cook the Aromatics:**
    - In the same pot, add the chopped onion. Cook until softened, about 5 minutes.
    - Stir in garlic and cook for another minute.
3. **Add Spices:**
    - Add cumin, coriander, paprika, cinnamon, ginger, turmeric, and cayenne pepper. Cook for 1-2 minutes, stirring constantly, until fragrant.
4. **Combine Ingredients:**
    - Return the browned lamb to the pot. Stir to coat with the spices.
    - Add diced tomatoes, broth, apricots, and honey. Bring to a simmer.
5. **Simmer:**

- Cover and reduce heat to low. Simmer for 1.5 to 2 hours, or until the lamb is tender and the flavors are melded. Stir occasionally.
6. **Finish:**
    - Stir in the sliced olives and toasted almonds. Cook for an additional 5 minutes.
7. **Serve:**
    - Garnish with chopped fresh cilantro or parsley.
    - Serve over couscous or rice.

Enjoy your rich and aromatic Moroccan Lamb Tagine!

Ratatouille

Ingredients:

- **1 eggplant**, diced
- **1 zucchini**, sliced
- **1 red bell pepper**, chopped
- **1 yellow bell pepper**, chopped
- **1 onion**, chopped
- **3 cloves garlic**, minced
- **1 can (14.5 oz) diced tomatoes** (or 2 cups fresh tomatoes, chopped)
- **1/4 cup olive oil**
- **1 tsp dried thyme**
- **1 tsp dried basil**
- **1/2 tsp dried oregano**
- **Salt and freshly ground black pepper**, to taste
- **Fresh basil** or **parsley**, for garnish

Instructions:

1. **Prepare the Vegetables:**
   - Dice the eggplant and sprinkle with salt. Let it sit for 30 minutes to draw out excess moisture. Rinse and pat dry.
2. **Cook the Vegetables:**
   - Heat olive oil in a large skillet or Dutch oven over medium heat.
   - Add onion and cook until softened, about 5 minutes.
   - Stir in garlic and cook for another 1 minute.
3. **Add Eggplant:**
   - Add the eggplant to the skillet and cook, stirring occasionally, until it starts to soften, about 5 minutes.
4. **Add Other Vegetables:**
   - Add the zucchini, bell peppers, and diced tomatoes. Stir in thyme, basil, oregano, salt, and pepper.
5. **Simmer:**
   - Reduce heat to low, cover, and simmer for 20-30 minutes, or until the vegetables are tender and flavors are melded.
6. **Finish and Serve:**
   - Adjust seasoning if needed. Garnish with fresh basil or parsley.

Enjoy your vibrant and hearty Ratatouille!

Burrata with Tomatoes and Basil

Ingredients:

- **1 ball Burrata cheese**
- **2 cups cherry tomatoes**, halved (or 1 large tomato, sliced)
- **1/4 cup fresh basil leaves**
- **2 tbsp extra virgin olive oil**
- **1 tbsp balsamic vinegar** (optional)
- **Salt and freshly ground black pepper**, to taste

Instructions:

1. **Prepare the Tomatoes:**
   - Arrange cherry tomatoes (or tomato slices) on a serving platter. Sprinkle with a pinch of salt and pepper.
2. **Add Burrata:**
   - Gently place the Burrata cheese in the center of the tomatoes.
3. **Add Basil and Drizzle:**
   - Scatter fresh basil leaves around the Burrata and tomatoes.
   - Drizzle with olive oil and balsamic vinegar if using.
4. **Serve:**
   - Serve immediately with crusty bread or as an appetizer.

Enjoy this fresh and creamy Burrata with Tomatoes and Basil!

Prawn Curry

Ingredients:

- **1 lb (450 g) prawns**, peeled and deveined
- **2 tbsp vegetable oil**
- **1 large onion**, finely chopped
- **3 cloves garlic**, minced
- **1 tbsp fresh ginger**, minced
- **2 tbsp curry powder** (or to taste)
- **1 tsp ground cumin**
- **1/2 tsp turmeric**
- **1/2 tsp paprika**
- **1 can (14.5 oz) diced tomatoes**
- **1 cup coconut milk**
- **1/2 cup chicken or vegetable broth**
- **1 tbsp tomato paste**
- **1 tsp sugar** (optional)
- **Salt and freshly ground black pepper**, to taste
- **Fresh cilantro**, chopped (for garnish)

Instructions:

1. **Cook the Aromatics:**
   - Heat vegetable oil in a large pan over medium heat.
   - Add onion and cook until softened and golden, about 5-7 minutes.
   - Stir in garlic and ginger, cooking for another 1-2 minutes.
2. **Add Spices:**
   - Add curry powder, cumin, turmeric, and paprika. Cook for 1-2 minutes until fragrant.
3. **Build the Sauce:**
   - Stir in diced tomatoes, coconut milk, chicken broth, and tomato paste. Bring to a simmer.
   - Add sugar if using, and season with salt and pepper.
4. **Simmer and Add Prawns:**
   - Simmer the sauce for about 10 minutes to blend the flavors.
   - Add prawns and cook until they are pink and opaque, about 3-5 minutes.
5. **Finish and Serve:**
   - Garnish with fresh cilantro. Serve over rice or with naan bread.

Enjoy your delicious Prawn Curry!

French Onion Soup

Ingredients:

- **4 large onions**, thinly sliced
- **2 tbsp unsalted butter**
- **2 tbsp olive oil**
- **2 cloves garlic**, minced
- **1 tbsp all-purpose flour**
- **6 cups beef broth** (or a mix of beef and chicken broth)
- **1 cup dry white wine** (or additional broth)
- **1 tsp fresh thyme** (or 1/2 tsp dried thyme)
- **1 bay leaf**
- **Salt and freshly ground black pepper**, to taste
- **8 slices French baguette** or crusty bread
- **2 cups grated Gruyère cheese** (or a mix of Gruyère and Parmesan)

Instructions:

1. **Caramelize the Onions:**
    - In a large pot, melt butter with olive oil over medium heat.
    - Add onions and cook, stirring frequently, until they are deep golden brown and caramelized, about 30-40 minutes. Be patient; this step is key for flavor.
2. **Add Garlic and Flour:**
    - Stir in minced garlic and cook for 1 minute.
    - Sprinkle flour over the onions and stir to combine. Cook for 2 minutes to eliminate the raw flour taste.
3. **Build the Soup:**
    - Gradually add beef broth and white wine, scraping up any browned bits from the bottom of the pot.
    - Add thyme, bay leaf, salt, and pepper. Bring to a simmer.
4. **Simmer:**
    - Reduce heat to low and simmer the soup for 20-30 minutes to blend the flavors. Adjust seasoning if necessary.
5. **Prepare the Toast:**
    - While the soup is simmering, preheat the broiler.
    - Place baguette slices on a baking sheet and toast under the broiler until golden brown on both sides.
6. **Assemble and Broil:**
    - Remove bay leaf from the soup.
    - Ladle the soup into oven-safe bowls. Place a toasted baguette slice on top of each bowl and sprinkle with grated cheese.

- Place bowls under the broiler until the cheese is melted and bubbly, about 2-3 minutes.
7. **Serve:**
    - Carefully remove the hot bowls from the oven and serve immediately.

Enjoy your comforting and flavorful French Onion Soup!

Baked Ziti

Ingredients:

- 12 oz (340 g) ziti pasta
- 2 cups marinara sauce
- 1 cup ricotta cheese
- 1 1/2 cups shredded mozzarella cheese
- 1/2 cup grated Parmesan cheese
- 1 egg
- **2 cloves garlic**, minced
- 1/2 tsp dried oregano
- 1/2 tsp dried basil
- **Salt and freshly ground black pepper**, to taste
- **Fresh basil or parsley**, for garnish (optional)

Instructions:

1. **Preheat Oven:**
   - Preheat your oven to 375°F (190°C).
2. **Cook the Pasta:**
   - Cook the ziti pasta according to package instructions until al dente. Drain and set aside.
3. **Prepare the Cheese Mixture:**
   - In a bowl, mix ricotta cheese, egg, minced garlic, oregano, basil, salt, and pepper.
4. **Combine Pasta and Sauce:**
   - In a large bowl, combine the cooked pasta with 1 1/2 cups of marinara sauce.
5. **Assemble the Dish:**
   - Spread a thin layer of marinara sauce on the bottom of a baking dish.
   - Add half of the pasta mixture, then dollop with half of the ricotta mixture. Sprinkle with a third of the mozzarella cheese.
   - Repeat layers with remaining pasta, ricotta mixture, and top with the remaining mozzarella and Parmesan cheese.
6. **Bake:**
   - Cover with foil and bake for 20 minutes. Remove foil and bake for an additional 10 minutes, or until cheese is melted and bubbly.
7. **Garnish and Serve:**
   - Let it cool for a few minutes before serving. Garnish with fresh basil or parsley if desired.

Enjoy your delicious Baked Ziti!

Duck Confit

Ingredients:

- **4 duck legs**
- **4 cloves garlic**, minced
- **1 tbsp fresh thyme leaves** (or 1 tsp dried thyme)
- **1 tbsp fresh rosemary**, chopped (or 1 tsp dried rosemary)
- **1 tbsp kosher salt**
- **1 tsp black pepper**
- **1/2 tsp ground white pepper**
- **2 cups duck fat** (or substitute with olive oil if needed)

Instructions:

1. **Prepare the Duck:**
   - Pat duck legs dry with paper towels. Rub garlic, thyme, rosemary, salt, and peppers all over the duck legs.
2. **Marinate:**
   - Place duck legs in a dish, cover, and refrigerate for at least 12 hours or overnight to allow flavors to meld.
3. **Preheat Oven:**
   - Preheat your oven to 300°F (150°C).
4. **Cook the Duck:**
   - Rinse the seasoning off the duck legs and pat dry. Place the duck legs in a baking dish or Dutch oven, and pour duck fat over them until fully submerged. If using olive oil, make sure it's enough to cover the legs.
5. **Slow Cook:**
   - Cover and bake in the preheated oven for 2.5 to 3 hours, or until the meat is tender and easily pulls away from the bone.
6. **Crisp the Skin:**
   - Remove duck legs from the fat and pat dry. Heat a skillet over medium-high heat and cook duck legs, skin-side down, until the skin is crispy and golden, about 5-7 minutes.
7. **Serve:**
   - Serve the duck confit with your choice of sides, such as roasted potatoes, vegetables, or a salad.

Enjoy your tender and flavorful Duck Confit!

Spicy Tuna Tartare

Ingredients:

- **8 oz (225 g) fresh tuna**, finely diced
- **1 avocado**, diced
- **2 tbsp soy sauce**
- **1 tbsp sesame oil**
- **1 tbsp Sriracha** (adjust to taste)
- **1 tsp rice vinegar**
- **1 tsp freshly grated ginger**
- **1 green onion**, finely chopped
- **1 tbsp chopped cilantro** (optional)
- **1 tsp sesame seeds** (optional, for garnish)
- **Tortilla chips** or **crackers**, for serving

Instructions:

1. **Prepare the Tuna:**
    - Place diced tuna in a bowl.
2. **Mix the Dressing:**
    - In a separate bowl, whisk together soy sauce, sesame oil, Sriracha, rice vinegar, and grated ginger.
3. **Combine Ingredients:**
    - Gently fold the dressing into the tuna. Add green onion and cilantro, mixing gently.
4. **Serve:**
    - Spoon the tuna mixture onto a serving plate or bowl. Top with diced avocado and sprinkle with sesame seeds if using.
5. **Accompaniments:**
    - Serve with tortilla chips or crackers.

Enjoy your flavorful and spicy Tuna Tartare!

Stuffed Mushrooms

Ingredients:

- **12 large mushrooms**, stems removed and chopped
- **2 tbsp olive oil**
- **1 small onion**, finely chopped
- **2 cloves garlic**, minced
- **1/2 cup breadcrumbs**
- **1/4 cup grated Parmesan cheese**
- **1/4 cup cream cheese**, softened
- **2 tbsp fresh parsley**, chopped
- **1/4 tsp dried thyme**
- **Salt and freshly ground black pepper**, to taste

Instructions:

1. **Prepare the Mushroom Caps:**
   - Preheat oven to 375°F (190°C). Arrange mushroom caps on a baking sheet.
2. **Cook the Filling:**
   - Heat olive oil in a skillet over medium heat. Sauté chopped mushroom stems, onion, and garlic until softened, about 5 minutes.
3. **Combine Ingredients:**
   - In a bowl, mix sautéed vegetables with breadcrumbs, Parmesan cheese, cream cheese, parsley, thyme, salt, and pepper.
4. **Stuff the Mushrooms:**
   - Spoon the filling into each mushroom cap, pressing it down gently.
5. **Bake:**
   - Bake for 15-20 minutes, or until mushrooms are tender and the tops are golden brown.
6. **Serve:**
   - Serve warm as an appetizer or side dish.

Enjoy your delicious Stuffed Mushrooms!

Chicken Cacciatore

Ingredients:

- **4 chicken thighs** and **4 chicken drumsticks** (or 8 pieces of chicken)
- **2 tbsp olive oil**
- **1 onion**, chopped
- **2 cloves garlic**, minced
- **1 red bell pepper**, sliced
- **1 green bell pepper**, sliced
- **1 cup mushrooms**, sliced
- **1 can (14.5 oz) diced tomatoes**
- **1/2 cup dry white wine** (or chicken broth)
- **1/2 cup chicken broth**
- **1/4 cup tomato paste**
- **1 tsp dried oregano**
- **1 tsp dried basil**
- **1/2 tsp dried rosemary**
- **Salt and freshly ground black pepper**, to taste
- **1/4 cup chopped fresh parsley** (for garnish)

Instructions:

1. **Brown the Chicken:**
   - Heat olive oil in a large skillet or Dutch oven over medium-high heat.
   - Brown chicken pieces on all sides. Remove and set aside.
2. **Cook the Vegetables:**
   - In the same skillet, add onion, garlic, and bell peppers. Sauté until softened, about 5 minutes.
   - Add mushrooms and cook for an additional 2 minutes.
3. **Add the Sauce:**
   - Stir in diced tomatoes, white wine, chicken broth, tomato paste, oregano, basil, rosemary, salt, and pepper. Bring to a simmer.
4. **Simmer:**
   - Return chicken to the skillet, submerging it in the sauce. Cover and simmer for 30-40 minutes, or until the chicken is cooked through and tender.
5. **Serve:**
   - Garnish with fresh parsley and serve over pasta, rice, or with crusty bread.

Enjoy your hearty and flavorful Chicken Cacciatore!

Creamy Tomato Basil Soup

Ingredients:

- **2 tbsp olive oil**
- **1 large onion**, chopped
- **3 cloves garlic**, minced
- **2 cans (14.5 oz each) diced tomatoes** (or about 6 cups fresh tomatoes, peeled and chopped)
- **2 cups chicken or vegetable broth**
- **1 cup heavy cream**
- **1 tsp dried basil** (or 1 tbsp fresh basil, chopped)
- **1 tsp sugar** (optional, to taste)
- **Salt and freshly ground black pepper**, to taste
- **Fresh basil leaves**, for garnish (optional)

Instructions:

1. **Cook the Aromatics:**
    - Heat olive oil in a large pot over medium heat.
    - Add chopped onion and cook until softened, about 5 minutes.
    - Stir in minced garlic and cook for another minute.
2. **Add Tomatoes and Broth:**
    - Stir in the diced tomatoes and their juice. Add the chicken or vegetable broth.
    - Bring to a simmer and cook for 15-20 minutes to let the flavors meld.
3. **Blend the Soup:**
    - Using an immersion blender, blend the soup until smooth. (Alternatively, you can carefully transfer the soup in batches to a blender and blend until smooth.)
4. **Add Cream and Seasonings:**
    - Return the soup to the pot if using a blender. Stir in heavy cream and dried basil. Add sugar if needed to balance the acidity. Season with salt and pepper to taste.
5. **Heat Through:**
    - Simmer the soup gently for an additional 5 minutes to heat through and allow the flavors to combine.
6. **Serve:**
    - Ladle the soup into bowls and garnish with fresh basil leaves if desired. Serve with crusty bread or a grilled cheese sandwich.

Enjoy your creamy and comforting Tomato Basil Soup!

Grilled Octopus

Ingredients:

- **1 large octopus** (about 2 lbs), cleaned
- **1/4 cup olive oil**
- **2 cloves garlic**, minced
- **1 lemon**, juiced
- **1 tsp smoked paprika**
- **1 tsp dried oregano**
- **Salt and freshly ground black pepper**, to taste
- **Lemon wedges**, for serving
- **Fresh parsley**, chopped, for garnish

Instructions:

1. **Pre-Cook the Octopus:**
   - Bring a large pot of salted water to a boil. Add the octopus and simmer for about 45-60 minutes, or until tender. Test with a fork; it should easily pierce the meat.
   - Remove from the pot and let cool. Once cool enough to handle, cut the tentacles off.
2. **Marinate:**
   - In a bowl, mix olive oil, garlic, lemon juice, smoked paprika, oregano, salt, and pepper.
   - Toss the octopus tentacles in the marinade and let them sit for at least 30 minutes, or up to 2 hours in the refrigerator.
3. **Grill:**
   - Preheat your grill to medium-high heat.
   - Grill the octopus tentacles for about 3-4 minutes per side, or until nicely charred and crisped up.
4. **Serve:**
   - Transfer the grilled octopus to a serving plate.
   - Garnish with fresh parsley and lemon wedges.

Enjoy your flavorful and perfectly grilled octopus!

Enchiladas Verde

Ingredients:

For the Filling:

- **2 cups cooked chicken**, shredded (or use pork or beef)
- **1 cup shredded cheese** (cheddar or Monterey Jack)
- **1/2 cup chopped onion**
- **1/2 cup fresh cilantro**, chopped
- **1 cup sour cream** (optional)

For the Sauce:

- **1 lb tomatillos**, husked and rinsed
- **1 small onion**, chopped
- **2 cloves garlic**, minced
- **1-2 jalapeños**, seeded and chopped (adjust to taste)
- **1 cup chicken or vegetable broth**
- **1 tsp ground cumin**
- **1/2 tsp dried oregano**
- **Salt and freshly ground black pepper**, to taste
- **2 tbsp vegetable oil**

For Assembling:

- **12 corn tortillas**
- **1 cup shredded cheese** (for topping)
- **Fresh cilantro**, chopped (for garnish)

Instructions:

1. **Prepare the Sauce:**
    - Preheat oven to 375°F (190°C).
    - In a large skillet, heat vegetable oil over medium heat. Add onions and cook until softened, about 5 minutes.
    - Add garlic, tomatillos, and jalapeños. Cook until tomatillos are soft, about 10 minutes.
    - Transfer the mixture to a blender or food processor, add chicken broth, cumin, oregano, salt, and pepper. Blend until smooth. Return to the skillet and simmer for 5-10 minutes. Adjust seasoning if needed.
2. **Prepare the Filling:**
    - In a bowl, mix shredded chicken, cheese, chopped onion, and cilantro.
3. **Assemble the Enchiladas:**

        - Heat tortillas in a dry skillet or in the oven until pliable.
        - Dip each tortilla in the tomatillo sauce, then spoon some of the chicken mixture onto the tortilla. Roll up and place seam-side down in a baking dish.
4. **Top and Bake:**
        - Pour remaining tomatillo sauce over the rolled tortillas. Sprinkle with additional cheese.
        - Bake for 20-25 minutes, or until cheese is melted and bubbly.
5. **Serve:**
        - Garnish with fresh cilantro and serve with sour cream if desired.

Enjoy your delicious Enchiladas Verde!

Shrimp Fettuccine Alfredo

Ingredients:

- **8 oz (225 g) fettuccine pasta**
- **2 tbsp olive oil**
- **1 lb (450 g) shrimp**, peeled and deveined
- **2 cloves garlic**, minced
- **1 cup heavy cream**
- **1 cup grated Parmesan cheese**
- **1/4 cup chopped fresh parsley**
- **Salt and freshly ground black pepper**, to taste

Instructions:

1. **Cook the Pasta:**
   - Cook fettuccine according to package instructions until al dente. Drain and set aside.
2. **Cook the Shrimp:**
   - Heat olive oil in a large skillet over medium heat.
   - Add shrimp and cook for 2-3 minutes per side, or until pink and opaque. Remove shrimp from the skillet and set aside.
3. **Make the Alfredo Sauce:**
   - In the same skillet, add minced garlic and cook for 1 minute until fragrant.
   - Pour in heavy cream and bring to a simmer. Cook for 3-4 minutes, stirring occasionally, until the cream has thickened slightly.
   - Reduce heat to low and stir in Parmesan cheese until melted and smooth. Season with salt and pepper.
4. **Combine and Serve:**
   - Add cooked fettuccine and shrimp to the sauce. Toss to coat the pasta and shrimp in the Alfredo sauce.
   - Stir in chopped parsley.
5. **Serve:**
   - Serve immediately, garnished with additional Parmesan and parsley if desired.

Enjoy your rich and creamy Shrimp Fettuccine Alfredo!

Stuffed Acorn Squash

Ingredients:

- **2 acorn squashes**
- **2 tbsp olive oil**
- **1/2 cup onion**, chopped
- **2 cloves garlic**, minced
- **1/2 cup quinoa** (or couscous, rice, or farro)
- **1 cup vegetable or chicken broth**
- **1/2 cup dried cranberries** (or raisins)
- **1/2 cup chopped walnuts** (or pecans)
- **1/2 cup crumbled feta cheese** (or goat cheese)
- **1/4 cup fresh parsley**, chopped
- **1 tsp ground cumin**
- **1/2 tsp dried thyme**
- **Salt and freshly ground black pepper**, to taste

Instructions:

1. **Preheat Oven:**
   - Preheat your oven to 375°F (190°C).
2. **Prepare the Squash:**
   - Cut the acorn squashes in half lengthwise and scoop out the seeds.
   - Brush the cut sides with olive oil and season with salt and pepper.
   - Place the squash halves cut-side down on a baking sheet and roast for 25-30 minutes, or until tender.
3. **Cook the Quinoa:**
   - While the squash is roasting, rinse the quinoa under cold water.
   - In a medium saucepan, bring the vegetable or chicken broth to a boil.
   - Add quinoa, reduce heat to low, cover, and simmer for 15 minutes or until the quinoa is cooked and the broth is absorbed. Fluff with a fork and set aside.
4. **Prepare the Filling:**
   - In a skillet, heat olive oil over medium heat. Add onion and cook until softened, about 5 minutes.
   - Stir in garlic and cook for another 1 minute.
   - Add cooked quinoa, dried cranberries, chopped walnuts, feta cheese, parsley, cumin, thyme, salt, and pepper. Mix well to combine.
5. **Stuff the Squash:**
   - Turn the roasted squash halves cut-side up.
   - Spoon the quinoa mixture into each squash half, packing it in gently.
6. **Bake:**
   - Return the stuffed squash to the oven and bake for an additional 10 minutes to heat through.
7. **Serve:**
   - Garnish with additional parsley if desired and serve warm.

Enjoy your flavorful and nutritious Stuffed Acorn Squash!

Beef and Broccoli Stir-Fry

Ingredients:

For the Marinade:

- 1/4 cup soy sauce
- 2 tbsp oyster sauce
- 1 tbsp hoisin sauce
- 1 tbsp cornstarch
- 1 tbsp brown sugar
- 1 tbsp **rice vinegar** (or white vinegar)
- 1 tsp sesame oil
- 1/2 tsp garlic powder
- 1/2 tsp ground ginger

For the Stir-Fry:

- 1 lb (450 g) **beef sirloin** or **flank steak**, thinly sliced against the grain
- 2 tbsp **vegetable oil** (divided)
- **3 cups broccoli florets**
- **1 red bell pepper**, sliced (optional)
- **1 onion**, sliced
- **3 cloves garlic**, minced
- **1 tbsp fresh ginger**, minced
- **1/2 cup beef broth** (or water)
- **2 tsp cornstarch** mixed with 2 tsp water (for thickening)
- **Cooked rice**, for serving

Instructions:

1. **Marinate the Beef:**
   - In a bowl, combine soy sauce, oyster sauce, hoisin sauce, cornstarch, brown sugar, rice vinegar, sesame oil, garlic powder, and ground ginger.
   - Add the sliced beef and toss to coat. Let marinate for at least 15 minutes, or up to 1 hour in the refrigerator.
2. **Cook the Broccoli:**
   - Heat 1 tablespoon of vegetable oil in a large skillet or wok over medium-high heat.
   - Add broccoli florets (and red bell pepper if using) and stir-fry for 3-4 minutes until bright green and slightly tender. Remove from the pan and set aside.
3. **Cook the Beef:**
   - In the same skillet, add the remaining tablespoon of vegetable oil.

- Add the marinated beef and stir-fry until browned and cooked through, about 3-5 minutes.
4. **Add Aromatics:**
    - Add garlic and ginger to the pan with the beef and cook for an additional 1-2 minutes until fragrant.
5. **Combine and Thicken:**
    - Return the broccoli (and bell pepper) to the pan.
    - Pour in beef broth and bring to a simmer.
    - Stir in the cornstarch mixture to thicken the sauce, cooking for 1-2 minutes until the sauce has thickened.
6. **Serve:**
    - Serve the beef and broccoli stir-fry over cooked rice.

Enjoy your flavorful and satisfying Beef and Broccoli Stir-Fry!

Lobster Roll

Ingredients:

- **1 lb (450 g) lobster meat**, cooked and chopped
- **1/4 cup mayonnaise**
- **2 tbsp unsalted butter**
- **1 tbsp lemon juice**
- **1 tbsp fresh chives**, chopped (or parsley)
- **1 celery stalk**, finely chopped
- **1 tsp Dijon mustard**
- **Salt and freshly ground black pepper**, to taste
- **4 hot dog buns** or **split-top rolls**
- **Lettuce leaves** (optional, for garnish)

Instructions:

1. **Prepare the Lobster Meat:**
   - If not already cooked, cook lobster tails in boiling salted water for about 8-10 minutes. Let cool, then remove the meat from the shells and chop into bite-sized pieces.
2. **Make the Lobster Mixture:**
   - In a bowl, combine mayonnaise, lemon juice, Dijon mustard, chives, celery, salt, and pepper.
   - Gently fold in the lobster meat, mixing until well combined. Adjust seasoning if needed.
3. **Prepare the Buns:**
   - Heat butter in a skillet over medium heat. Brush the outside of each hot dog bun with melted butter.
   - Toast the buns in the skillet until golden brown and crispy, about 2-3 minutes per side.
4. **Assemble the Rolls:**
   - Place a lettuce leaf (if using) inside each toasted bun.
   - Spoon the lobster mixture into each bun.
5. **Serve:**
   - Serve immediately, garnished with additional chives if desired.

Enjoy your delicious and classic Lobster Roll!

www.ingramcontent.com/pod-product-compliance
Lightning Source LLC
LaVergne TN
LVHW081618060526
838201LV00054B/2305